ILLUSTRATIONS

The illustrations in this book were drawn by Laurie Ferguson and are original half-tone pencil drawings of New Jersey subjects. The source materials were old paintings, lithographs, photos, drawings and models. Some arc composite drawings from several other works and some are originals by the artist. They have been placed throughout the book so as to add interest and graphic information for the reader.

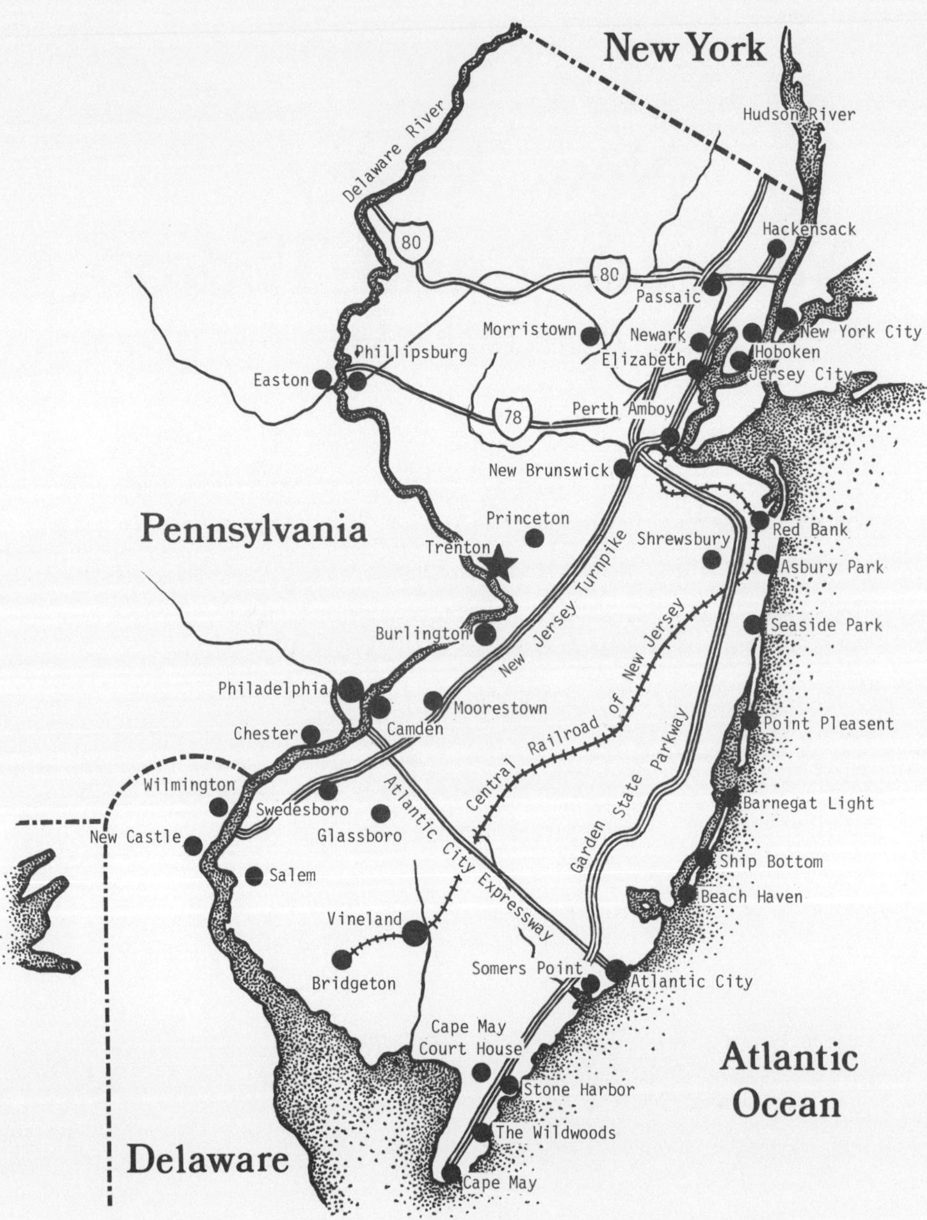

New York
Hudson River
Delaware River
Hackensack
80
80
Passaic
Morristown
Newark
New York City
Phillipsburg
Elizabeth
Hoboken
Jersey City
Easton
78
Perth Amboy
New Brunswick
Pennsylvania
Princeton
Shrewsbury
Red Bank
Trenton
New Jersey Turnpike
Asbury Park
Burlington
Seaside Park
Philadelphia
Central Railroad of New Jersey
Moorestown
Chester
Camden
Point Pleasant
Wilmington
Atlantic City Expressway
Garden State Parkway
Barnegat Light
Swedesboro
New Castle
Glassboro
Ship Bottom
Salem
Beach Haven
Vineland
Somers Point
Atlantic City
Bridgeton
Cape May
Court House
Atlantic
Ocean
Stone Harbor
The Wildwoods
Delaware
Cape May

New Jersey
Yesterday and Today

By
Phillip Fair and Ted Rabold

Illustrated By
Laurie Ferguson

PENNS VALLEY PUBLISHERS
Harrisburg, Pennsylvania
1981

PREFACE

New Jersey: Yesterday and Today has been planned to help students learn about the founding, settling, growth and development of the state of New Jersey in modern times.

The book has been designed primarily to be used as a classroom textbook but it can also be used by individual students as a resource for research.

Each chapter has been organized in an easily readable manner which contains much factual information. Following each of the chapters are ten questions which are intended to help students recall facts and information discussed in the text. In addition, there are activities and suggestions for further research to help students achieve a deeper level of involvement and a greater understanding of the topic about which they have just read.

New Jersey's story is a significant part in the saga of America's growth. It is our hope that this book will help the reader gain a clearer perspective of New Jersey's role in America's past as well as its place in America's future.

CONTENTS

CHAPTER 1

Words you need to know

sagas	*Whitutuck*	*Unclachtigo*
migrated	*clans*	*wigwams*
Lenni Lenape	*Minsi*	*scalp lock*
Algonkians	*Unami*	

NEW JERSEY'S FIRST PEOPLE

Have you ever stood in a forest or a woods far away from houses and highways and airports and factories? If you have you probably have some idea of what it might have been like to live in New Jersey hundreds of years ago.

Before people from Europe came to live in the area we now call New Jersey the land belonged to the Indians. The Indians did not build cities or highways or have great farms. They hunted and fished and grew a few kinds of crops in the soil. We often forget that there ever were Indians here. But we are reminded of New Jersey's first people when we look carefully at a map of our state and see that many towns and rivers have Indian names. Who were these first people? Where did they come from? How did they live and what happened to them? The answers to these questions make-up the first part of the story of the history of New Jersey.

Studying the history of the first people who lived in New Jersey is not easy. History is a record of things which happened in the past. But, the Indians did not know how to write as we do. Many of the things we know about them come from stories called *sagas*. These sagas were told over and over again by Indians who remembered them. Parts of the sagas were written in pictures on bark or animal skins. They were saved for those who came later to read and remember them.

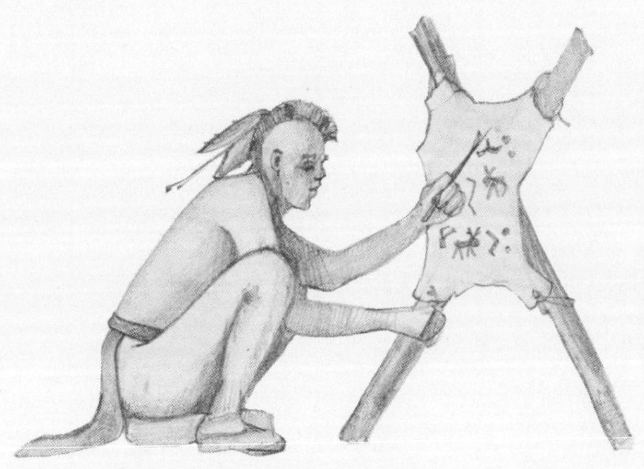

The sagas tell that thousands of years ago, groups of Indians moved or *migrated* across a bridge of land from Asia to North America. In time, these groups spread over much of what is now the western part of Canada and the United States. One of these groups called themselves the *Lenni Lenape*. The name meant "original people". They

2

The Land Bridge between Asia and America

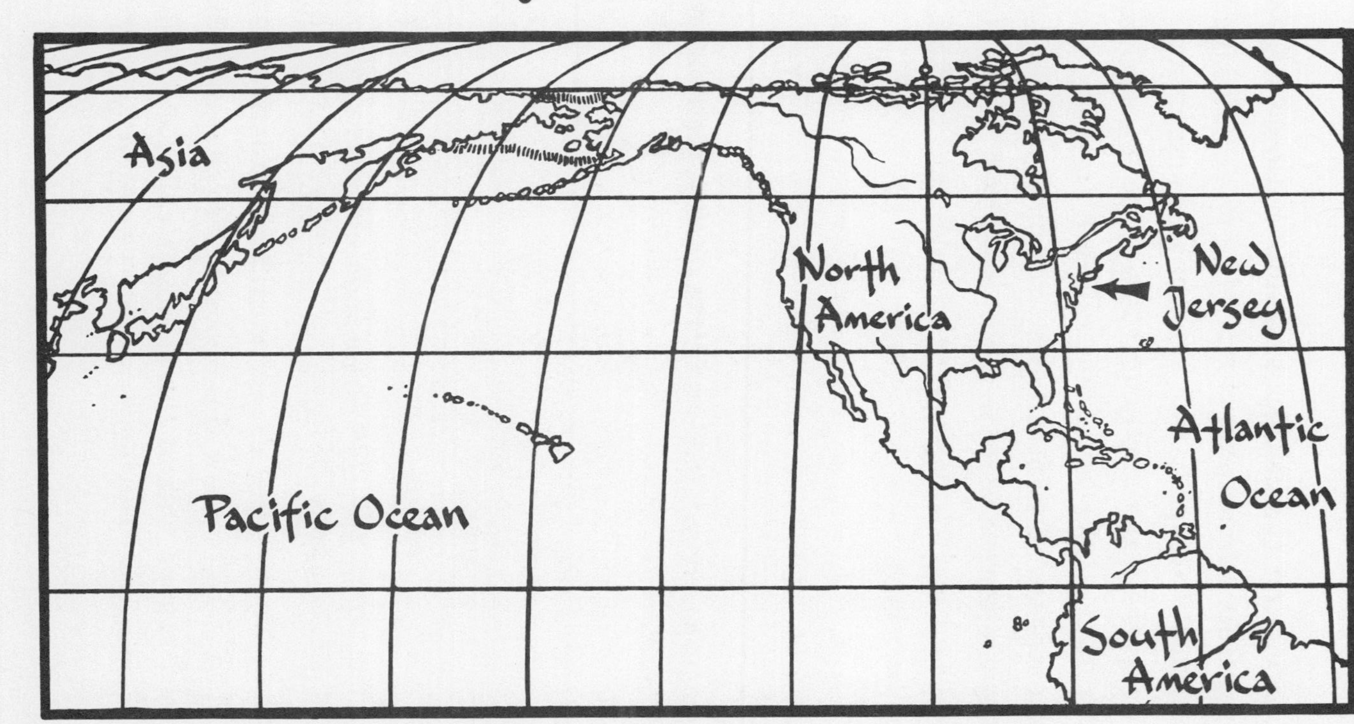

were a part of a larger group of Indians known as the *Algonkians*. Over many years the Lenni Lenape moved east until they came to a land which lay between a fast flowing river and the ocean. The Indians called the river *Whitutuck* which means "rapid stream". Later settlers from Europe gave it the name Delaware by which it is known today.

The Lenni Lenape were divided into three tribes or *clans* which lived in different parts of what are now the states of New Jersey and Pennsylvania. In the northern mountains lived the *Minsi* or Wolf clan. The name Minsi meant "people of the stony country". In what is now the middle of New Jersey near the city of Trenton lived the *Unami* or Turkey clan. Their name meant "people down the river". The third clan lived in the south near the Atlantic ocean and were called the *Unclachtigo* or Turtle clan. Their name meant "people who live near the ocean".

The Lenni Lenape lived in villages along the Delaware River. Their houses were called *wigwams*. Wigwams were made by sticking small trees into the ground, bending down the tops and tying them together to form a frame. The frame was covered with bark, animal skins or thick layers of grass. There were no windows and only one door. The floor of the wigwam was dirt and there was a place for a fire in the middle. In the top of the wigwam there was a hole for the smoke to escape. Since the wigwam was not very comfortable, the Lenni Lenape did not spend much time indoors. They used their house for sleeping and for shelter in bad weather.

The Lenni Lenape found many things to eat in the woods, rivers and along the seacoast. They hunted animals in the woods with bow and arrows. They caught fish in the rivers with spears and nets. They dug for clams and oysters along the shore. Huge piles of oyster shells have been found near the ocean as proof of this. They also grew vegetables in small gardens near their villages. They liked corn, beans and squash. Wild berries and nuts were added to many of the things they ate.

The clothing of the Lenni Lenape was simple but comfortable. In the summer they wore very little. When colder weather came, however, both men and women wore shirts and pants made of animal skins. The skins were sewed together using hair or tough grass. They also made blankets and coats of skins and bird feathers. Since bird feathers keep out water these coats would be used as rain coats.

The Indians liked jewelry. They wore arm bands, necklaces, and earrings made of animal teeth, colored stones and shells. Both men and women painted their faces.

They used colored clay, wood ashes and berries. Red was a favorite color. Men and boys usually shaved their heads using sharp stones. They would leave a strip of hair down the center of their heads called a *scalp lock*. This hair was rubbed with animal fat to make it stand up. Often several eagle feathers were worn at the back of the head.

The family was very important to the Lenni Lenape. Every member of the family had to do work. Children were almost never punished when they were little. However, they were expected to learn fast and to grow up quickly. For a boy, part of growing up meant spending several nights alone in the forest without food. When he returned to the village he was supposed to have become a man.

Everything the Lenni Lenape used in life came from nature. Because of this they believed in a Great Spirit which controlled everything. Beautiful things in nature like flowers and sunsets were made by the Great Spirit. They believed that each Indian was watched over by his own friendly spirit. When they became sick it was because their friendly spirit was angry at them.

More than 300 years ago, white people from Europe began coming to what is now the state of New Jersey. They found the Lenni Lenape living in their villages near a great river which they called the Delaware. The white people did not understand the Indians language. They called them Delawares because they lived near a river of that name.

The Lenni Lenape were peaceful people who did not like war. They often worked to keep wars from happening be- tween other tribes. They believed in sharing everything they owned. When a stranger came to one of their villages he was always given food. But there were many differences in the way Indians and Europeans lived. These differences made it hard for the Lenni Lenape to stay peaceful.

QUESTIONS

1. Why did the Indians of New Jersey use sagas?
2. From where did the Indians migrate?
3. What did the Indians in New Jersey. call themselves? What does that name mean?
4. How many clans did the Indians divide into? What were their names?
5. What was the name of the type of house the Indians of New Jersey lived in?
6. What type of food did the Indians of New Jersey eat?
7. What did they use to make clothing?
8. Give three examples of ways Indians of New Jersey decorated themselves.
9. What did a boy have to do before becoming a man?
10. What did the settlers from Europe call the Indians of New Jersey?

ACTIVITIES

1. On a map of the world, trace the route Indians may have followed to New Jersey.
2. Build a diorama or draw a picture of a Lenni Lenape village.
3. Write a story using the Indians' sign language.

ADVANCED RESEARCH

1. Locate on a map cities, towns, and rivers that have names which remind us the Lenni Lenape once lived in New Jersey.
2. What did the Lenni Lenape use for money and how did they make it?

CHAPTER II

Words you need to know

Europeans	*settlers*	*Quaker*
explorers	*founded*	*proprietors*
colonies	*mosquitoes*	
journal	*Puritans*	

EXPLORERS AND EARLY SETTLERS

The Lenni Lenape lived in the land we call New Jersey for many many years without knowing that across the Atlantic Ocean in Europe there lived people who were very different from them. These *Europeans* had learned to sail ships, powered by wind, across the ocean. Almost five-hundred years ago, European *explorers* began to sail along the shores of New Jersey. Imagine how surprised the Indians must have been when they saw these ships and the men on board them. They were as different to the Indians as creatures from another planet would be to us. They wore strange clothes and spoke strange languages which the Indians could not understand. These people even carried frightening weapons such as steel swords and guns which the Indians had never seen. The explorers were looking for places where other Europeans could come to live. Such places were called *colonies*. The explorers liked what they found in New Jersey and soon the Indians had many new neighbors.

HENRY HUDSON AND CAPTAIN MEY

The first Europeans to see New Jersey were John Cabot and Giovanni da Verrazano. They did not do much exploring but what they saw interested other explorers.

The first European to explore New Jersey was Henry Hudson. He sailed his ship, called the Half-Moon, along New Jersey's beaches and up the river which was later called the Hudson River. Henry Hudson was from England but he was working for the government of Holland. One of the men on board the Half-Moon kept a *journal* of what he saw on the trip. As the ship sailed along the New Jersey coast he wrote that it was "a pleasant land to see". Later some of the ship's crew went ashore and met with the Indians. Most of the Indians were friendly but some were afraid of these "white men". One of the sailors was killed by an Indian arrow and he was buried at a place called Sandy Hook.

Another explorer from Holland who left his name in New Jersey was Captain Cornelius Mey. He explored the Delaware River and the bay at its mouth. He named the long strip of land or cape which sticks into the bay for himself. Today we spell it differently but still call it Cape May.

DUTCH COLONISTS

The explorers were followed to the land they had found by *settlers* or colonists. The first colonists were from Holland and were called the Dutch. The Dutch colonists began to settle along both the Hudson and the Delaware Rivers. Their most important settlement was across the Hudson River in what is now called New York but some of them lived in New Jersey. They called their colony New Netherland.

The Dutch traded with the Indians and began to clear the trees from the land so that they could begin farms. They even started a copper mine and built a road over one hundred miles long to carry the copper ore from the mine to boats on the Hudson River.

The first town in New Jersey was *founded* by the Dutch in the year 1660. It was called Bergen and was located where Jersey City is today. The town was built to protect the people from attacks by the Indians. All around the town was a high wooden wall. This was necessary because the settlers and the Indians disagreed about who owned the land and fighting had broken out between them. The fighting continued for many years. Finally, a peace treaty was signed with the help of an old Indian chief named Oratam.

The Dutch were very hard working people who used the soil of New Jersey to raise good crops of grain, vegetables and fruit. They had large families and built stone houses and churches which can still be seen today in parts of northern New Jersey.

SWEDISH COLONISTS

Another group of settlers from a country called Sweden tried to start a colony in New Jersey about the same time as the Dutch. The Swedes, as they were called, tried to build several settlements along the Delaware River. One of their leaders was a huge man named Johan Printz. He was seven feet tall and was said to weigh nearly four hundred pounds. Printz built a fort on a hill overlooking the Delaware River near what is today the town of Salem. He felt the fort was necessary to protect his settlement against the Dutch and Indians. His greatest enemy, however, seemed to be swarms of *mosquitoes* whose bites could be very uncomfortable. Johan Printz called the place Fort Elfsborg but his soldiers nicknamed it "Mosquito Castle".

Some Swedes also settled further north in a place they called Raccoon. More than two-hundred years ago the name of Raccoon was changed to Swedesboro. This is one of the few reminders that we have today of the fact that there was once a Swedish colony in New Jersey. This is because not many Swedes came to live in New Sweden, as it was called, and the Swedish colonists were soon outnumbered by colonists from other countries.

NEW JERSEY GETS ITS NAME

The settlers who were to outnumber both the Dutch and the Swedes came from England. England already had colonies in Massachusetts and Virginia and did not want other countries to control the land in between. In the year 1664, King Charles of England gave all this land to his brother, the Duke of York. The Duke sent soldiers to capture the Dutch colony of New Netherland. The soldiers renamed the colony New York in honor of the Duke. The Duke of York then gave the land between the Hudson and the Delaware Rivers to two of his friends. One of these friends, Sir George Carteret, had been born on an island near England called Jersey. In honor of Sir George, the Duke insisted that the land he had given his friends be called New Jersey.

ENGLISH COLONISTS

English settlers began to arrive in New Jersey very quickly after the colony was under the control of the English soldiers. One of the first settlements was Elizabethtown. It was located between the Raritan and Passaic Rivers and was later called simply Elizabeth. The first settlers bought the land from the Indians. The price was some cloth, two coats, two guns, two kettles, ten bars of lead and twenty handfuls of gun powder. This was not really very much to pay for so much land. The Indians probably did not understand that they could never use the land again. The Indians were slowly losing New Jersey to the Europeans.

Many of the English people who settled in the northern part of the colony were *Puritans* from Massachusetts and Connecticut. The Puritans had their own way of worshipping God and were trying to find a place to live where they did not disagree with other people. They came to New Jersey hoping to find such a place.

In the year 1666, a Puritan leader named Robert Treat brought thirty families to a small town on the Passaic River. It was soon called Newark, in honor of a town of the same name in England. One year later, Newark had a population of about three-hundred and fifty people.

Other towns including Piscataway and Woodbridge were founded by groups of Puritans. These towns were alike in many ways. The Puritans were very strict and believed in strong punishments. Most towns had public whipping posts for punishing people who broke the rules of the town. Staying out after nine o'clock at night could mean a whipping. A thief could have the letter T branded on the back of his hand so that others would know of his crime.

In the center of these early New Jersey towns were meetinghouses which were used as churches, schools and places for the townspeople to gather and to make decisions about how to run their town. Pieces of open land or greens were set aside in the center of the towns as places for the town's soldiers to practice marching. These greens were also used by the cows and sheep of the town as pastures. Some of these greens can still be found in the center of New Jersey's modern cities. Military Park in Newark was once a village green.

WEST NEW JERSEY

The south western part of New Jersey was settled by a group of English people called *Quakers*. The Quakers were also looking for a place to live peacefully and worship God freely. They were not popular in England because they refused to serve in the army and they would not swear an oath of loyalty to the King.

    The first Quakers to reach what they called West New Jersey, sailed up the Delaware River in a ship called the Griffin in the year 1675. They went ashore and founded the town of Salem. The name Salem came from the Hebrew word Sholem which means peace. Another group of Quakers arrived in West New Jersey two years later and started the town of Burlington further up the Delaware River. During their first winter these people lived on deer meat and corn which was given to them by friendly Indians. The Quakers got along well with the Indians. This was because they believed that all men should be treated as equals.

Have you been noticing how some of the familiar places in New Jersey got their names? Some were named for places from which people had come. Some were named for ideas which people believed in and many were named for the people who first settled them. New Jersey's capital city today is an example of this. The first settlers were mainly farmers. However, as more settlers arrived there was a need for other kinds of business. The farmers needed a place to grind their grain into flour. A mill for this purpose was built at a place in the Delaware River called, "The Falls". That was because the river was rough and fast there and the fast flowing water could be used to turn the mill wheel. Later, a village grew up around the mill. When some of the land was sold to a man named Trent, people started calling the place Trent's Town and then Trenton.

NEW JERSEY BECOMES ONE COLONY

For about forty years, New Jersey was really two colonies. One was called West New Jersey and the other was called East New Jersey. In both colonies the people who controlled things were men called *proprietors*. The proprietors made the rules and tried to charge the colonists rent or taxes for the property on which they lived. The colonists did not like these taxes and many refused to pay them. There were many angry meetings in both colonies. Finally, the government of the King of England decided that it would be easier to control one colony instead of two. In the year 1702, the colonies of East and West New Jersey were united under one government. In time, the colonists of New Jersey would come to dislike the government of the King of England as much as they had disliked the government of the proprietors.

QUESTIONS

1. What do you think the Indians of New Jersey thought about the explorers from Europe? Why?
2. Why did the explorers come to this new land?
3. Who was the first explorer of New Jersey and which government did he work for?
4. Where were the first colonists in New Jersey from and what were they called?

5. Who was the man who built Fort Elfsborg and what country was he from? What did the soldiers call Fort Elfsborg?

6. How did New Jersey get its name?

7. Who were the English people from Massachusetts and Connecticut who lived in Northern New Jersey?

8. Why did the people come from Massachusetts and Connecticut?

9. Why did the Quakers come to New Jersey? Why didn't they stay in England?

10. Why did East New Jersey and West New Jersey become one colony?

ACTIVITIES

1. On a map of the world, find where Holland, Sweden and England are located. Trace the route taken by these people to one of their settlements in New Jersey.

2. On a map of New Jersey, label the Atlantic Ocean, Hudson River, Delaware River, Cape May, Jersey City, Swedesboro, Elizabeth, Passaic River, Newark, Piscatawny, Woodbridge, Salem, Burlington and Trenton.

ADVANCED RESEARCH

1. Find out more about the Puritans and Quakers. How were they the same? How were they different?

2. Try to find how other New Jersey cities got their name.

CHAPTER III

Words you need to know

ministers	*document*	*retreat*
goods	*Declaration of Independence*	*victory*
boycott	*commanding*	*defeated*
revolution	*volunteered*	*crept*
independence	*professional*	*diary*

NEW JERSEY AND THE WAR FOR INDEPENDENCE

TEA PARTY AT GREENWICH

If your home had been in the town of Greenwich, New Jersey in the year 1774, you might have been very surprised to look out of your window on a night in December. Indians were dancing around a huge fire in the middle of the town's main street! If you had been able to get a closer look, however, you would probably have realized that these were not real Indians but "White Men" dressed as Indians. The fire they were dancing around was burning boxes filled with tea. What was happening? Why were men, pretending to be Indians, burning tea on the main street in Greenwich? Tea was a popular drink in colonial New Jersey. Did they dislike tea? Let us look at the reasons behind the Greenwich Tea Party of 1774.

The King of England ruled the colony of New Jersey for more than seventy years. During this time many colonists had come to live in New Jersey and the other English colonies in America. As the years went by these people began to think of themselves as Americans and Jerseymen rather than Englishmen. They did not like many of the rules which the King and his *ministers* wanted them to obey. They were most unhappy about the taxes which the King's government expected them to pay. The taxes had to be paid on many of the *goods* which the colonists bought from England including tea. The English thought this was fair because they sold the goods to the colonists at very low prices. The colonists thought the taxes were unfair because they did not have any chance to discuss them and to agree or disagree.

The colonists objected to the taxes by refusing to buy many of the English goods. This is called a *boycott*. The boycott worked and the English took away nearly all of the taxes except the one on tea. This satisfied some of the colonists but not all of them. In Boston, Massachusetts, another of the English colonies, a group of men went on board an English ship which was carrying tea. They broke open the boxes holding the tea and threw it into Boston Harbor. News of this "Boston Tea Party", as it was called, soon reached the other colonies, including New Jersey. The men of Greenwich, whom we read about earlier, decided to have a "Tea Party" of their own.

THE WAR BEGINS

The boycotts and the "tea parties" were the beginning of what became a long war between England and the colonies. It was called the *Revolution* or the War for *Independence*. This was because the colonists had declared that they wanted independence or freedom from England. On July 4, 1776 they signed a *document* called the *Declaration of Independence*. The declaration explained their reasons for wanting to be free.

George Washington was the *commanding* general of the Colonial Army. He was a very good general but it was not easy to make a good army in a short time. The men in his army were farmers and workmen who had *volunteered* to fight for independence. They had very little training as soldiers. The British Army was made up of well trained *professional* soldiers. In the fall of 1776, General Washington was forced to *retreat*, with his army, across New Jersey and into Pennsylvania. The British Army controlled New York and New Jersey. Many colonists gave up hope that the war could ever be won. General Washington knew he had to win a *victory* if the Revolution was to go on.

Many important battles between the colonists and the English or the British, as they were called, took place in New Jersey. This was partly because New Jersey lay between two of the most important cities in the colonies, New York and Philadelphia. For this reason New Jersey had been called the "Crossroads of the Revolution".

SURPRISE AT TRENTON

The British hired soldiers from Germany to do some of their fighting for them. A force of these soldiers, called Hessians, was camped in Trenton on the New Jersey side of the Delaware River. On Christmas Night, 1776, Washington led the American Army across the Delaware. They made the crossing in 40 foot boats that were normally used to carry iron ore down the river. It was dark and large pieces of ice, floating in the river, banged into the boats making the crossing even more dangerous. By the time the army of two thousand four hundred men reached the New Jersey side it began to snow and sleet. Some of the soldiers had no shoes so they wrapped cloth rags around their feet. They had to walk nine miles to Trenton without talking or making any noise so the Hessians would not know they were coming.

At eight o'clock in the morning, on the day after Christmas, the attack began. In Trenton, the Hessians had been celebrating Christmas and were completely surprised by the American attack. The Hessian officer in charge had been warned several times to be on the lookout for an attack. He had decided, however, that it would be impossible for General Washington to get his army across the Delaware River and attack Trenton. He had spent the night eating and playing cards and was fast asleep when the fighting began. The Battle of Trenton lasted about forty-five minutes. When it ended the Hessian commander was dead and over nine hundred of his men had been taken prisoner by the Americans. With their prisoners, the American Army recrossed the Delaware to the Pennsylvania side.

About one week later, just after New Year's Day in 1777, the American Army crossed the Delaware River into New Jersey again. This time the British Army, led by Lord Cornwallis, was waiting for them near Trenton. It seemed certain that the Americans would be *defeated*, but General

Washington again used surprise. Some of his soldiers stayed behind at Trenton to make noise and to keep the fires of the camp burning. The rest of the army quietly crept out of the camp and circled around the British soldiers. They attacked the British from behind near the college town of Princeton. By the time Lord Cornwallis realized his mistake the Americans had won another victory. Nassau Hall on the campus of Princeton College was the center of much fighting. The marks made by cannon balls can still be seen on the walls of the building today. As a result of the battle at Princeton, the British were forced to retreat back to New York. The Americans now controlled New Jersey and General Washington moved his army to Morristown where they camped for the winter.

THE BATTLE OF MONMOUTH

The war for Independence continued and gradually the Americans began to win. One other important battle took place in New Jersey and once again, George Washington was the hero. The British Army had spent the winter of 1778 in the warm comfort of the city of Philadelphia. In June, the British commander, General Clinton, was ordered to move his men north to New York. Clinton set out for New York with eleven thousand men and fifteen hundred wagons to carry their baggage and supplies. As the army began to march across New Jersey an early summer heat wave raised temperatures to over one-hundred degrees. This was especially uncomfortable for the British soldiers because they wore heavy winter uniforms and carried backpacks weighing over fifty pounds.

George Washington decided to attack the British Army as it marched to New York. The American Army had been carefully trained during the winter by a German General named Baron Von Steuben. They were much better prepared to fight the professional British soldiers than they had been earlier. Washington thought his army could defeat the British and, perhaps, end the war. He placed General Charles Lee in command of the American forces. General Lee was sure that the British Army was much stronger than the Americans and that it could easily defeat his forces.

The two armies met near Monmouth Courthouse. Soon after the battle began, and even though the Americans were fighting well, Lee ordered his soldiers to retreat. At that moment, General Washington appeared on the scene. He was very angry when he saw what General Lee had done. He quickly ordered the retreat stopped and then rode his horse into the middle of the battle to urge the American soldiers to attack.

The Battle of Monmouth lasted all day. Many were killed on both sides but the British Army did manage to get away to New York. Had General Lee been more willing to attack it might have resulted in a great American victory. It was the longest and the largest battle of the entire war. The British Army never really returned to New Jersey.

MOLLY PITCHER

With the American Army that day in Monmouth was a woman named Mary or "Molly" Hays. Her husband John was a soldier. She and other wives of soldiers had traveled with the army to help in whatever way they could. As the battle continued, men began to faint in the one-hundred degree heat. Molly filled a pitcher with water from a nearby spring. All day long she carried it back and forth to the wounded and thirsty men. In order to get her attention the men called out, "Molly! Pitcher!", "Molly! Here!" In this way she got the name Molly Pitcher. Later, when her husband John was wounded by a British bullet, Molly took his place helping to load and fire a cannon. After the battle, George Washington praised Molly for her bravery and her help. Today, a monument in her honor can be seen on the Monmouth Battlefield.

A COLD WINTER AT MORRISTOWN

Many people know that George Washington and his army spent a long and cold winter at a place called Valley Forge in Pennsylvania during the War of Independence. Not as many people know that the American Army spent three winters in New Jersey. One of those, the winter of 1779 and 1780, was colder and probably more difficult for the men of the army than the one spent at Valley Forge. During that winter the American Army camped at Morristown while the British Army stayed in New York. It was the worst winter in nearly one-hundred years in New Jersey. The Hudson River froze solid in spots so that people could walk across it. There were twenty-eight snow storms during the winter. Snow drifts were as much as five and six feet deep. The soldiers lived in tents and wooden huts in Jockey Hollow near Morristown. Many had almost no clothes and had to sleep on straw covered ground with only one blanket. Sometimes the snow completely covered their tents. The snow made it almost impossible for supplies to get through to the camp. This meant that the soldiers had almost nothing to eat and some were close to starving to death. One officer wrote in his *diary* that, "At one time the soldiers ate every kind of horse food but hay".

General Washington and his wife Martha lived in the house of a woman named Mrs. Ford in Morristown. Many of the famous leaders of the War for Independence came to meet with General Washington in the Ford's house. Often these meetings took place in the kitchen. It was the only warm room in the house because a fire was always burning in the fireplace there.

Today the Ford House in Morristown and the soldier's camp in Jockey Hollow are part of a national historical park. You can visit them and try to get a feeling for what it must have been like to live through the winter of 1779–1780. Perhaps you can also think about what kept the men in the American Army going. They were cold, sick and hungry and many were going to be killed in battle. It is important to remember that they were fighting for an idea which was more important to them than their own comfort. The idea, of course, was the freedom of their country. But it took much suffering and bravery to make it possible.

A NEW NATION

The War for Independence ended on September 3, 1783. The government of the King of England agreed that New Jersey and the other colonies no longer belonged to England. They were now part of an independent country, the United States of America. The people were free to choose their own leaders. They were also free to make their own laws and to decide which taxes they would pay.

It took time, but the new nation grew and became strong. New Jersey grew with it and became one of its most important states. As the years passed, many more people came from around the world to make their homes in the United States of America. They came for many reasons and from many places. One of their most important reasons for coming, however, was to share in the freedom won by the soldiers and leaders of the War for Independence.

QUESTIONS

1. Where in New Jersey did the tea party of 1774 take place?
2. Why did the colonists in New Jersey stage a tea party?
3. What document did the colonists write to England telling that they wanted to be free?
4. Who was the commanding general of the Colonial Army?
5. Why was New Jersey called the "Crossroads of the Revolution"?
6. Who did the colonial army surprise and defeat at Trenton the day after Christmas?

7. General Washington attacked the British soldiers as they marched from Philadelphia to New York. Where did the attack take place?
8. How did Molly Pitcher get her name?
9. What was the main problem General Washington's army had at Morristown?
10. The colonies won the War for Independence. What did that mean to the relationship between England and the colonies?

ACTIVITIES

1. Make a diorama, picture or write a story about the cold winter at Morristown.
2. Draw a map of New Jersey and show where the battles in New Jersey took place.
3. From what you have learned in this chapter, write what might have been in the Declaration of Independence.

ADVANCED RESEARCH

1. Research the Boston Tea Party and describe the differences and similarities between the Boston and Greenwich Tea Parties.
2. Read the Declaration of Independence. List the reasons the colonists wanted to be free.

CHAPTER IV

Words you need to know

transportation	*suspension*	*locomotive*
raw materials	*bulky*	*invest*
travelers	*towpath*	*passenger*
fording	*engineering*	*commuter*
ferry	*inclined plane*	*resort*
link	*barge*	

TRANSPORTATION IN NEW JERSEY: THEN AND NOW

As part of a new nation, New Jersey grew quickly. One of the most important things which grew in New Jersey was the way in which the people moved themselves and goods around the state. The ways in which things are moved is called *transportation*. Without good transportation New Jersey would be a very different place. Businesses and industries would not be able to get the *raw materials* they need to make things and they would not be able to send their finished products to far away places. The state's workers would not be able to get to or from their jobs. Students would not be able to go to New Jersey's schools. People from other states would not be able to visit the many interesting and relaxing places to be found in New Jersey.

EARLY PATHS AND ROADS

The Lenni Lenape traveled about New Jersey on narrow footpaths. They did not know about the wheel and had no wagons or carts. This meant that their footpaths were only wide enough for one person to walk on them at a time. When the first European settlers arrived they also traveled on the Indians' footpaths. Gradually, these paths became wider as the settlers drove cows over them and began to use carts and wagons. In time the paths began to be called roads. They did not look much like the roads that we use today. The roads were muddy when it rained and dusty in dry weather. They were filled with holes and stones. Sometimes as many as eight horses were needed to pull heavily loaded wagons through the mud and over the hills. In 1752, before the War of Independence, a trip by wagon between New York and Philadelphia, across New Jersey, took almost three days. The ride could also be painful. After being bounced and shaken in a wagon with no springs for three days, many *travelers* were so sore that they could not walk.

CROSSING RIVERS

One of the problems early travelers had was crossing streams and rivers. If the stream was shallow they could splash across on foot. This was called *fording* a stream.

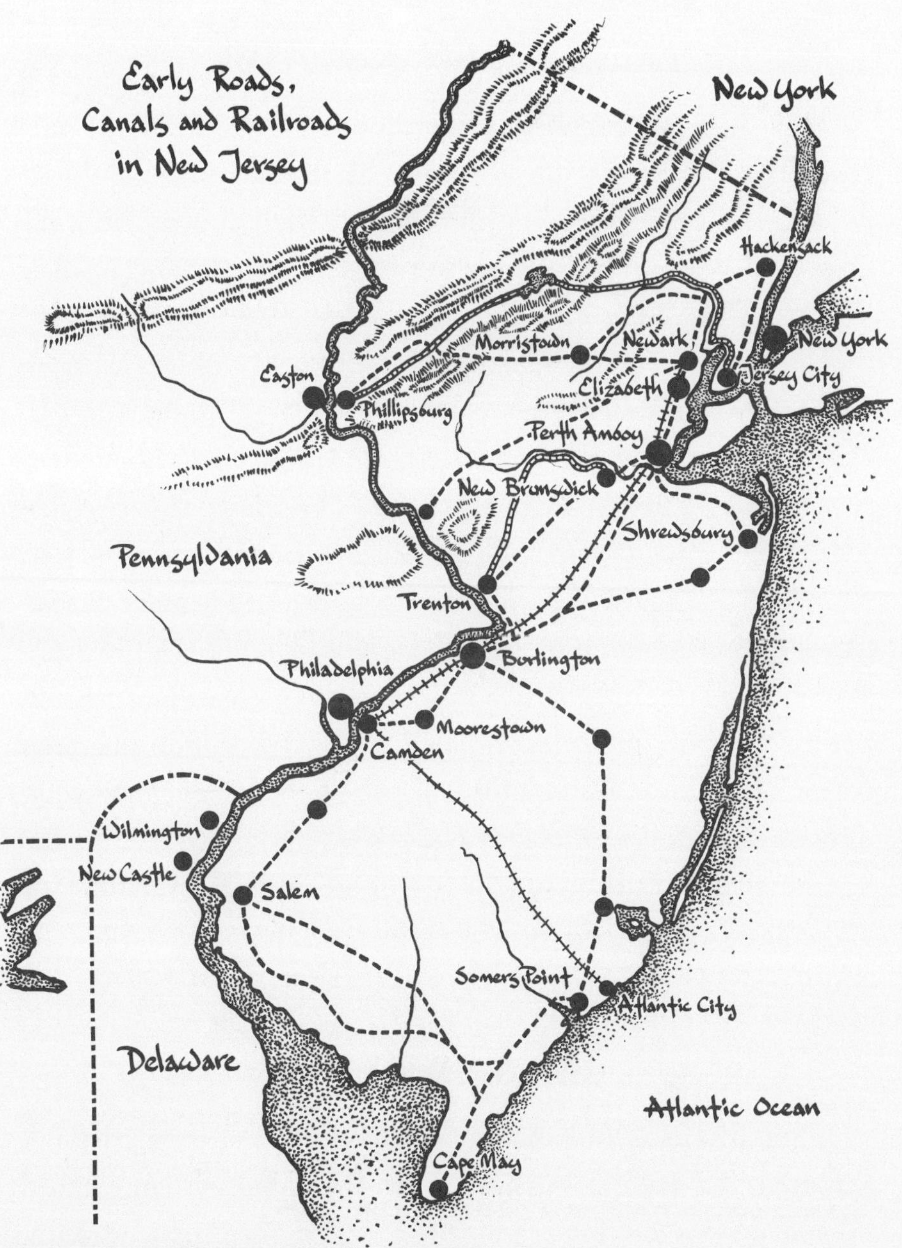

Early Roads,
Canals and Railroads
in New Jersey
New York
Hackensack
New York
Morristown
Newark
Jersey City
Easton
Elizabeth
Phillipsburg
Perth Amboy
New Brunswick
Shrewsbury
Pennsyldania
Trenton
Philadelphia
Burlington
Moorestown
Camden
Wilmington
New Castle
Salem
Somers Point
Atlantic City
Delaware
Atlantic Ocean
Cape May

However, larger rivers like the Delaware, the Passaic, the Raritan and the Hudson could not be forded. There were no bridges so when a traveler came to one of these rivers he had to wait for a *ferry*. The ferries were run by boatmen who charged money to take travelers across rivers. The early ferries were nothing more than rowboats and often the travelers had to help row. Later ferries were large enough to carry horses and wagons. Later still, cars, trucks and even trains were carried across rivers by ferry.

Bridges finally replaced the ferries across most of the rivers and *linked* New Jersey to other states. The first bridge across the Delaware River to Pennsylvania was built at Trenton in 1806. It was made from stone and wood and was more than one-thousand feet long. Most of the early bridges were built by companies which charged money to travelers who wanted to cross. At least they did not have to wait for ferries any longer.

Today New Jersey has more bridges of different kinds than almost any state in the nation. Modern steel and concrete bridges cross all of New Jersey's waterways. They make it possible for a traveler to go almost anywhere in very little time. The George Washington Bridge crosses the Hudson River at Fort Lee. It is one of the longest *suspension* bridges in the world. More than seventy-five million cars, trucks and buses cross it each year.

TURNPIKES AND TOLL ROADS

Just as it cost money to use the first bridges, travelers often had to pay to use the early roads. A company would build or improve a road and then it would collect money, or tolls, from the travelers who used it. At the places where the tolls were to be collected a long wooden pole was put across the road to stop the traveler. This pole was called a "pike". When the traveler paid his toll the pike was turned out of the way. He could then continue on his journey. Because the pole was used in this way such roads were called turnpikes. We use this same word today for many roads which charge tolls. The New Jersey Turnpike, which runs across the state from Camden to Newark is one example. Another modern toll road in the state is the Garden State Parkway. It runs from New Jersey's border with New York in the north to the state's southern tip at Cape May.

CANALS

As New Jersey's industries continued to grow there was a need for a transportation system which could carry large amounts of heavy and *bulky* goods. Things like coal, iron, bricks and sand were too heavy to carry in large quantities in wagons pulled by horses. Other states were building canals and some people in New Jersey decided that canals would be a good idea too.

A canal is like a road of water. A ditch or channel must be dug in the earth. Then the channel must be filled with water from a nearby river or lake. Boats used on the canals could have engines to make them go but most canal boats were pulled by mules or horses. The mules were guided by a man or boy who walked along beside the canal on a small road called a *towpath*.

New Jersey had two important canals. The Morris Canal was called one of the *"engineering* wonders of America"*. It stretched nearly one-hundred miles from Jersey City, on the Hudson River, to Phillipsburg, on the Delaware River. High mountains lay between these two cities. In order to cross these mountains the canal boats had to climb over nine-hundred feet from Newark Bay to Lake Hopatcong. Then they had to go down the other side of the mountains to Phillipsburg. But how does a boat climb mountains?

The canal builders constructed *inclined planes* to raise and lower the boats over the mountains. An inclined plane was like a huge sliding board with tracks on it. When a boat came to one of the planes a small carriage was placed under it and it was pulled up the inclined plane by ropes. Wheels, turned by water power, did the pulling. There were twenty-three of these inclined planes on the Morris Canal. The largest was at Hopatcong and was one-thousand and six-hundred feet long.

It took nearly five days for a boat to cross New Jersey on the Morris Canal. Towns along the way like Dover and Boonton grew as the canal boats brought coal to their iron works. New towns grew along the canal with names like Port Colden and Port Murray. They had places to eat and stay for the canal boatmen. Canal boat captains sometimes had their families living on the canal boats with them. The children could play and fish in the canal, help with work on the boat and sometimes drive the mules. In the winter, when the canal froze, the children would go to school in the towns along the canal.

The other New Jersey canal was called the Delaware and Raritan. It ran from Bordentown, on the Delaware River, through Trenton and then to New Brunswick, on the Raritan River. The D&R, as it was called, followed an almost level route and did not need inclined planes to cross the mountains. By 1850, steam boats were pushing barges of coal through the D&R bound for New York City. A *barge* could cross New Jersey on the D&R in about twenty hours.

For more than seventy years both of these New Jersey canals carried thousands of tons of coal and other goods. However, in the winter the canals often froze solid and could not be used. It also cost a great deal of money to keep them in working order. The canals finally stopped being used. The thing which really made them unnecessary was the coming of the railroads.

THE RAILROADS

In 1824, Colonel John Stevens built the first steam *locomotive* in America. He called it a "Steam Waggon". To show people how it worked, Colonel Stevens built a circle of track beside his house in Hoboken. People did come to watch and to ride on the Waggon. They were amazed at its speed of twelve miles per hour. Colonel Stevens hoped that people would be so interested that they would want to *invest* some money in a railroad. He had permission from the state of New Jersey to build a railroad from New Brunswick to Trenton. But most people thought that a railroad was not a very good idea at that time. They were sure that it was too dangerous and would cost too much money.

Even though people did not listen to Colonel Stevens he continued to believe in the future of railroads. Several years later, his son, Robert, went to England. In England he had a man build a locomotive called the John Bull. The John Bull weighed ten tons. It was too heavy to run on the wooden rails then being used. Robert Stevens developed a new type of rail called the T-rail. It was made of iron and was strong enough to hold the John Bull. Robert also invented the hook-headed iron spike which fastens the rails to wooden ties. All of these inventions by Robert Stevens are still used on modern railroads.

Robert Stevens brought the John Bull back to New Jersey. In 1834 it began to pull trains carrying passengers between Camden and South Amboy. It traveled at a speed of thirty miles per hour. In six years it was possible to make the trip across New Jersey in about seven hours. The trip was not very comfortable and was not always safe. On one early trip the locomotive hit a pig which had wandered onto the tracks. The train jumped the track, rolled down a hill and several *passengers* were injured. Another danger in riding on an early railroad came from the sparks made by the wood burning locomotive. The sparks would land on the passengers and sometimes burn holes in their clothing. It was not wise to wear new clothes when you were riding on a train.

RAILROAD COMMUTERS

In spite of these dangers more railroads were built and New Jersey came to depend upon them for business and travel. The railroads changed the ways in which the people of New Jersey lived and worked. Many people worked in the great city of New York across the Hudson River from New Jersey. Many of these workers did not wish to live in the city. They liked the quiet towns and clean air that could be found in parts of New Jersey. The railroads made it possible for people to live in New Jersey and travel to work each day on the train. Towns grew up along the railroads in northern and central New Jersey. The people who used the trains in this way were called *commuters*. Many people still commute to work on New Jersey's railroads today.

In southern New Jersey, the railroads carried fruit and vegetables from towns like Woodbury and Millville to markets in larger cities. They also helped to bring people to the sea coast. In fact, some of the famous New Jersey *resort* towns got started because of the railroads.

A RAILROAD TO THE OCEAN

In 1820, a young doctor named Jonathon Pitney came to Absecon Island on the coast. He loved the sand dunes, the ocean and the salt air. He believed that if people could visit places like Absecon Island more often less people would be sick. However, very few people lived there or came to visit. The roads were very poor and the trip took too much time. Dr. Pitney worked long and hard to convince people that a railroad was needed to bring visitors to Absecon Island. Finally, enough people agreed. It was felt, however, that a new name was needed for the town. A name that would make people think of the ocean. The name they decided upon was Atlantic City. Tracks were built from Camden and trains began to arrive in Atlantic City in 1854.

Visitors found they did enjoy the ocean and the salt air and kept returning for more. Atlantic City has been a famous resort ever since.

Transportation in New Jersey today is modern and fast. New Jersey's many forms of transportation have made the state a very busy place. People travel to and from jobs and vacations. They use automobiles, buses, trains and airplanes. Things manufactured in New Jersey can be transported anywhere in the United States and the world by trucks, trains and ships. Goods from around the world are unloaded from ocean going ships in Camden, Elizabeth, Bayonne and Newark. The goods are then carried on New Jersey's highways and railroads across the state and the nation. A good transportation system has made New Jersey one of the most important states in the country.

QUESTIONS

1. What does transportation mean? Give three examples of transportation in New Jersey.
2. How do businesses and industries use transportation?
3. What were the first roads in New Jersey and who made them?
4. Before there were bridges, how did the early travelers cross streams and rivers?

5. Where can one of the longest steel suspension bridges in the world be found. What is its name?

6. How did turnpikes get their names?

7. What were canals and how were they used?

8. Why was the Morris Canal called one of the engineering wonders of America?

9. What was the John Bull and what was invented because of it?

10. What helped Atlantic City become a vacation resort and why?

ACTIVITIES

1. On a map of New Jersey show and label where the following transportation routes were:
   a. The first bridge over the Delaware River.
   b. The George Washington Bridge.
   c. The New Jersey Turnpike.
   d. The Garden State Parkway.
   e. The Morris Canal.
   f. The Delaware and Raritan Canal.
   g. The route of the John Bull.
   h. The first railroad route to Atlantic City.

2. Draw a picture or make a diorama of transportation in New Jersey.

3. Pretend you lived in New Jersey in 1800. Describe your trip from Philadelphia to New York City.

ADVANCED RESEARCH

1. Some cities and towns began along transportation routes and others began because of industries. Try to find out why a city or town near where you live is located where it is.

2. Using a map of New Jersey, plan and describe a trip which will use water, railroad and automobile routes.

CHAPTER V

Words you need to know

industry	*ore*	*dyeing*
business	*bellows*	*textiles*
spout	*relaxation*	*manufactured*
harpoon	*refining*	*bogs*
blubber	*crude*	*harvested*
mineral	*laboratories*	*resources*

MAKING A LIVING IN NEW JERSEY
THE WAY IT USED TO BE

What do making wampum and hunting whales have in common with iron making and glass making? They are all examples of *industries* in which the people of New Jersey made their living at one time. An industry is a *business* which earns money by making or doing something for which people will pay. Today, New Jersey is a state of many industries. We will look more closely at a few of the industries which played a part in the growth of New Jersey.

WHALING

Cape May lies at the most southern point in New Jersey. On one side of the cape is the Atlantic Ocean. On the other is Delaware Bay. It was here that the New Jersey whaling industry started more than three-hundred years ago. Whalers, as those who caught whales were called, came to Cape May from New England. They built houses on a high hill overlooking Delaware Bay. When a lookout sighted a whale's *spout* he would call, "Thar she blows." The whalers would row out in small boats to where the whale was swimming. A man in the bow of the boat would try to stick an iron *harpoon* into the whale. This was the dangerous part. Whales were often fifty or sixty feet long. They could easily smash the small boats with a flip of their huge tails. Many whalers drowned when their boats were upset. If the boat did not upset, the whalers often got a long and fast ride. The harpoon was fastened to the boat by a rope. Sometimes the whale would try to swim out to sea towing the boat and the whalers behind him.

When the whale finally died its body would be pulled to the beach. There it was cut into pieces and the *blubber* was cooked in huge pots. From the blubber came whale oil. Several thousand gallons of whale oil could be made from a large whale. The whale oil was burned in lamps which people at that time used to light their homes. It could be sold for a great deal of money.

The whaling industry of Cape May ended as fewer and fewer whales came in the bay. The people had to find other ways to make a living near the ocean. Today New Jersey has many fishermen. They make their living by catching fish and clams which they sell for food. The whaling industry is only a memory in New Jersey.

MAKING WAMPUM

Another unusual industry in New Jersey's history was a factory which actually made money. This was not the sort of money we use today. It was a kind of money used by the Indians called wampum. Men who traded with the Indians gave them wampum in exchange for animal furs. Wampum was made by cutting and polishing the shells of clams and other "shellfish" which live in the ocean. Wampum came in many shapes and colors. There were beads, pipes and special shapes called moons.

In 1775, William Campbell settled in Park Ridge and began to make wampum. He would buy wagon loads of clams and he would invite his neighbors to come to a free clam feast. When the feast was over the clam shells would be gathered and made into wampum. Both William Campbell and his neighbors got something from the bargain. Campbell sold the wampum he made to Indian traders. Park Ridge became one of the only places in America where wampum was made.

The wampum business was continued by William Campbell's sons and grandsons for more than one-hundred years. Finally, the few Indians who were left stopped using wampum as money and another New Jersey industry came to an end.

IRON MAKING

Perhaps the most important of New Jersey's early industries was iron making. Iron is a *mineral* which comes from the ground. When the first settlers began moving into northern New Jersey the Indians showed them something they called "Blackstone." The stone was iron *ore*. It was already being used in other parts of the world to make metal tools. Now iron tools could be made in New Jersey. Iron ore mines were dug in many parts of New Jersey. Iron making took place in Shrewsbury, Batsto and Ringwood. However, until about one-hundred years ago, more iron ore was found in Morris County, New Jersey than in any other part of the United States.

Making iron required a large furnace. The furnace was made of stone. A very hot charcoal fire had to be kept burning in the furnace to melt the iron ore. The iron maker used the wood of many trees to keep the fires of his furnace going. The furnace was usually built near a fast flowing stream. The stream would turn a water wheel which worked a bellows. The *bellows* would blow air into the fire to make it hotter. When the iron ore melted, it would run out of the furnace into narrow holes dug in sand. As it cooled it would harden into bars which were called pigs. This kind of iron was called pig iron.

Pig iron could be made into many things. During the War for Independence, the iron works at Hibernia and Mount Hope made cannons and cannon balls for George Washington's army. In 1826, a young man from Newark named Seth Boyden invented a way to make iron that could be shaped more easily. This increased the number of things which could be made with iron.

Iron from New Jersey helped make the nation grow. Iron mills in Trenton made rails and wheels for the railroads. Railroad locomotives made in Patterson were used around the country. Iron beams, made in New Jersey, were used to strengthen the Capital Building in Washington, D.C.

About one-hundred years ago iron ore was found in other parts of the country. It was easier and cheaper to mine. Because of this cheaper ore most of the iron and steelmaking industry moved to other states. However, other industries took the place of ironmaking as New Jersey continued to grow.

GLASS MAKING

When colonists first settled in New Jersey they were not able to make many of the things they needed themselves. One of the things they had to buy from England in those early days was glass. This meant that glass was very special and expensive. In 1738, a man named Caspar Wistar opened the first successful glassmaking factory in America. It was located at Alloway, near Salem. Glass is made by heating sand in a furnace until the sand melts. Molten glass can then be shaped into many things by blowing air into it through a hollow pipe. Caspar Wistar had looked at the sand in Salem County and thought that it would be perfect for making good glass. He was right and another New Jersey industry was born.

Many people liked the glass that Caspar Wistar made and his glassworks soon became famous. Young men came to work and learn how to make beautiful glass objects at the Wistar Glass Works. Later they went on to start their own glass making businesses in other parts of New Jersey. One such business was started by seven brothers named Stanger. They opened a glassworks in a forest in Gloucester County in 1775. The town which grew up around this business is called Glassboro.

For many years, New Jersey supplied glass for the nation's bottles, jars, pitchers and windows. Between 1840 and 1860, one-third of all the glass made in the United States was made in New Jersey. Though not as important as it once was, glassmaking is still one of the state's many industries.

NEW JERSEY'S INDUSTRIES TODAY

We have seen some of the industries which helped New Jersey grow in the past. Now let us look at some of the many industries which New Jersey has today. We have already read, in an earlier chapter, about the importance of the transportation industry in the state. Thousands of people in New Jersey work at moving people and things. They help to unload ships on the docks and they drive trains, trucks and buses. The other industries of the state can be divided into three types. Those that make things, those that grow things and those which provide fun and *relaxation* for other people.

INDUSTRIES THAT MAKE THINGS

Many things are made in New Jersey today. There are more than twelve-thousand factories in the state. Many of these factories are found in the area around Newark, Elizabeth and Jersey City in the northeastern part of New Jersey. A number of factories are also found around Camden and Trenton along the Delaware River. If you look at a map of northeast New Jersey you will see that it is very crowded with towns and cities. Good transportation and many people have made this an important industrial area. It is impossible to talk about all of the industries but we will look at a few examples.

Oil *refining* is a large New Jersey industry. Oil refineries are found at Bayonne and Perth Amboy in the northeast. At a refinery, *crude* oil from the ground is made into gasoline and kerosene. Oil companies also have *laboratories* in these cities to test their products and try to find new uses for them.

There are many laboratories or research centers in New Jersey where engineers and scientists work to find better ways of doing things. Researchers in Nutley and Rahway have discovered new medicine. Engineers at a laboratory at Murry Hill invented the transistor. It made many of the radio and television sets of today possible. Transistors are important in computers.

At Rutherford, Summit and New Brunswick, drugs and medical supplies, like bandages, are made. They are supplied to doctors and hospitals across the United States. School books, like this one, are printed in Rockleigh, Hightstown and Englewood Cliffs. Cookies and crackers are baked and packaged in Fair Lawn.

Paterson is a city which has had many industries over the years. Some of the first factories in the United States were begun there along the Passaic River. Today one of the most important industries in Paterson is the making and *dyeing* of cloth or *textiles*.

At Bound Brook, factories make plastics, paint and insulation for buildings. Phillipsburg, on the Delaware River, is where heavy machinery is *manufactured*. Trenton is the state capital but it is also a city of industries. Many things are made there including steel wire and cables. The cables which support the George Washington Bridge were made in Trenton. Trenton is also famous for pottery and the manufacture of beautiful chinaware dishes and vases. The city's motto is "Trenton Makes-the World Takes."

Huge ships are built and repaired at Camden. Camden is also famous for producing food products, particularly canned soup. Another huge oil refinery can be found at Paulsboro. Ships from around the world unload their crude oil here. At Carney's Point one of the largest chemical manufacturing plants in the world is located.

These are just some of the industries found in New Jersey which make things.

FARMING

New Jersey is called the Garden State. This name refers to another kind of New Jersey industry, farming. The farmers of New Jersey grow many things. They grow more fruits and vegetables than anything else. The best area for growing vegetables in New Jersey is the southwestern part of the state. This includes the areas of

Cumberland, Salem, Gloucester and Burlington counties. Over fifty kinds of vegetables are grown here. Asparagus, spinach, green peppers, lima beans and tomatoes are the most common.

Blueberries and cranberries are grown in the wet and sandy areas in what is called the Pine Barrens. Cranberries must be grown underwater in *bogs*. When they are *harvested* they float to the surface and are gathered in large scoops.

Dairy cows are raised in Hunterdon and Sussex counties in the north. On farms in Monmouth and Cumberland counties, chickens produce millions of eggs each year. Flowers are another farm product. More orchids are grown in Middlesex County, New Jersey than in any other state in the nation.

The number of farms in New Jersey has grown smaller in recent years but farming is still one of the state's important industries.

THE JERSEY SHORE

Natural *resources* are things which nature has given us. People have found ways to make them useful. Some of New Jersey's greatest natural resources are the beaches of the Atlantic Ocean. These beaches and the cities along them have given New Jersey another important industry. It is called the resort industry. Millions of people travel many miles each summer to enjoy the sun, the sand and the water. Cities like Asbury Park. Atlantic City, Ocean City, Wildwood, Cape May and many others depend upon these visitors. Motels, hotels and restaurants are businesses where people stay and get things to eat. Recently, Atlantic City decided to try a new type of industry called casino gambling. It is hoped that this will bring more people to the businesses in that town. Many new hotels and restaurants are being built there.

We have seen that there are many different ways in which people make their living in New Jersey. Some of the old industries have disappeared but many new ones have taken their place. Industries keep changing as new products and new ways of doing things appear. The people of New Jersey have made changes and have kept their state growing.

QUESTIONS

1. What are making wampum and hunting whales examples of in New Jersey?
2. In what part of New Jersey was the whaling industry located?
3. Why were whales killed?
4. What was used to make wampum?
5. Why were iron furnaces usually built near fast flowing streams?
6. What was pig iron?
7. Describe how glass was made in early New Jersey.
8. Give three examples of industries in New Jersey which make things.
9. Why is New Jersey called the Garden State?
10. What is one of New Jersey's greatest and most popular natural resources?

ACTIVITIES

1. On a map of New Jersey, locate and label any five cities and the city where or near where you live. Off to the side of the map, list some products or industries which come from each of the cities.
2. On a road map, plan a trip to a resort which is at least fifty miles from where you live. Describe what routes you would take to get there.
3. Pretend you are a whaler. Describe in writing what happens after you have sighted a whale.

ADVANCED RESEARCH

1. Make a picture chart which shows the process of making a steel bar.
2. What are five of New Jersey's leading industries today?
3. Describe the process which cranberries go through to get on your table.

CHAPTER VI

Words you need to know

ancestor   *famine*   *plantations*
generation   *custom*   *ethnic*
immigrants   *recent*

THE PEOPLE OF NEW JERSEY

IMMIGRATION

Nearly seven and a half million people live in New Jersey today. They are people with *ancestors* from many parts of the world. Some have lived in the state for many *generations*. Others have come here only recently. An important part of the story of the United States and of New Jersey is the history of people coming here from other countries. Such people are called *immigrants*. Perhaps more immigrants have settled in New Jersey over the years than in any other state in the country. This may be because New Jersey is located between the two large port cities of New York and Philadelphia. Many immigrants arrived by boat in one of these cities. Some of them liked what they found in New Jersey and decided to live here.

It is not easy to leave your home in one country and to find a new home in another country. But for more than three hundred years people have been doing just that to come here. New Jersey had much to offer new immigrants and the immigrants had much to offer New Jersey.

EARLY IMMIGRANTS

As we read earlier, the Dutch and the Swedes were the earliest settlers in New Jersey. They might be considered the first immigrants. They were followed by the English. The English controlled the colony of New Jersey for more than one-hundred years. During that time many immigrants came from England. After the War of Independence, immigrants from England, Scotland and Wales continued to come to New Jersey. Later, large numbers of people came from Ireland and Germany. The Irish came because their country was hit by a terrible *famine*. Thousands of people starved to death. The Germans came to get away from wars which were sweeping their country. Both groups found jobs and homes in New Jersey.

LATER IMMIGRANTS

About one-hundred years ago immigrants from many other countries began to arrive in New Jersey. They came from Italy, Poland, Hungary, Russia, Greece and many other nations. These immigrants came for many reasons. They were poor and needed jobs. Friends and relatives who had come to America earlier had written them letters telling what a wonderful place it was to live. Some wanted to get away from countries where people did not like them and had been treating them unfairly. This was true for many

Jewish people. America was a place where they could find a job. It was also a place where they would be free to live as they wished.

ARRIVING IN AMERICA

A trip across the ocean by ship often took several weeks. Most immigrants did not have much money. They were forced to ride in the most uncomfortable part of the ship. They would be crowded together below decks where it was hot and noisy.

One of the first things many of the immigrants saw as their ship sailed into New York Harbor was the Statue of Liberty. The statue was a gift to the United States from the people of France in 1884. It became a symbol of the freedom which this country has always offered immigrants. Although the Statue of Liberty stands in New York harbor it is actually within the State of New Jersey. You can visit the statue by taking a boat from Liberty Park in Jersey City.

Near the Statue of Liberty is a place called Ellis Island. It is also inside New Jersey but it belongs to the United States government. Most new immigrants had to stop at Ellis Island before they could enter the United States. There they would be examined by doctors to see if they had any serious diseases. They would also be asked questions

about where they had come from and where they planned to go. When the doctors and the inspectors were satisfied, the immigrants were allowed to leave Ellis Island. They could then begin to look for new homes in the United States.

The immigrants were strangers in the new country. They often spoke different languages which made it hard for them to find jobs and places to live. For this reason they usually settled in places where they found other people who were like themselves. Sometimes whole towns were settled by one group. A group of German immigrants started Carlstadt in 1854. Italian farmers settled Hammonton before 1900. Nearly all of the people who lived in certain Italian villages came to live in Hammonton. This sometimes caused people to fear that the immigrants were not really interested in becoming Americans. By staying together as they did people were afraid the immigrants would turn the country into "Little Italies," "Little Polands" and "Little Germanies."

IMMIGRANTS BECOME AMERICANS

It took time but the immigrants began to show that they wanted to become Americans. They were proud of the countries where they came from but they worked hard to be part of America. Often the jobs immigrants did were things that no one else wanted to do. For example, they dug canals, laid tracks for the railroads, built roads, bridges and tunnels and they laid bricks and poured cement. They also worked in factories, steel and textile mills, shined shoes, made clothes, swept the streets, unloaded ships on the docks, and they picked fruits and vegetables on the farms. The immigrants worked long and hard and eventually many became citizens of the United States.

As the children of immigrants grew up and went to school they learned to speak English and learned American *customs*. It became hard to tell the difference between the people who had come from different countries. The immigrants wanted to save and remember some of the old ways. They did not want the young people to forget who their ancestors were and from where they had come. Today, many people remember that their ancestors once came to New Jersey from other lands. On holidays and special occasions they sing the songs, eat the foods, wear the clothes and dance the dances of those lands.

RECENT IMMIGRANTS

People still come to New Jersey. Many of the most *recent* immigrants are from the Spanish speaking countries of South America. Many are from Puerto Rico and Cuba. People from Puerto Rico are not really immigrants from another country. Puerto Rico is part of the United States and its people are United States citizens. However, they are moving to another part of the country.

Another group of recent immigrants are from a country called Portugal which is located in Europe. These people are called Portugese and speak a language which is also called Portugese. Newark, Elizabeth, Harrison and Kearny, New Jersey all have large Portugese populations.

These newer immigrants have suffered some of the same hardships which the earlier immigrants suffered. They have not always been treated fairly. However, they have come to find the same things that immigrants have been finding in New Jersey for many years. They too are helping to make New Jersey better.

BLACKS IN NEW JERSEY

Another group of people who settled in New Jersey in its earliest days were blacks. Black people were different from other immigrants. Not only was their skin darker but they had not come to New Jersey because they wanted to come. They had come because they were forced to come here as slaves.

Black slaves were brought to New Jersey and other colonies from Africa. Their trip across the ocean was even worse than the trips taken by the immigrants from Europe.

The slave traders who brought them fastened their feet to the ship's decks with chains. When they arrived in America they were sold to the person who would pay the most money for them. Sometimes, members of the same family were sold to different owners. Children were separated from their parents.

The slaves were forced to work all their lives for their masters. Sometimes a kind master would set a slave free after many years of work. This did not happen very often. Many people thought that black people were not equal to white people. They saw no reason to treat them the same way they treated others.

After the War for Independence some people began to realize that slavery was not right. If Americans had fought a war for freedom, they asked, how could they think that it was all right to keep other people as slaves? In New Jersey a law was passed in 1804 which slowly brought slavery to an end. It did not free all slaves at once but no more slaves could be brought into the state. However, in the southern United States slavery continued for many years. There people had come to depend upon slaves to do much of the work on *plantations*.

THE UNDERGROUND RAILROAD

Slaves from those southern states often ran away from their masters. They would come north to New Jersey, New York and Pennsylvania. From there they moved to Canada where they could be free. In parts of New Jersey people who thought slavery was wrong helped these runaway slaves to escape. They would hide them in their houses and barns during the day. At night they would lead them to another hiding place further north. This escape system was called the Underground Railroad. It was not a real railroad but it worked very much like one. Camden and New Brunswick were important points on the Underground Railroad and many runaway slaves passed through these towns.

CIVIL WAR AND FREEDOM

A Civil War was finally fought between the states of the north and the south. When the war ended the northern states had won. People were no longer allowed to own slaves anywhere in the country. The laws of the United States were changed to say that black people were equal to others. However, for many years after the Civil War many people did not follow these laws. Black people were often not treated fairly. In New Jersey and other states, blacks had not been allowed to go to school. They could not get good jobs and were often very poor.

In the last sixty years many more black people have come to live in New Jersey. They came from the southern states to cities like Newark where they hoped to find jobs. Like the immigrants from other countries they often found jobs that other people did not want to do. At times when fewer jobs were available blacks were often the first to lose their jobs.

Today things are changing slowly. More and more blacks have been able to go to schools and colleges. This has meant they can get better jobs and start their own businesses. The future looks better but there is still a need for more understanding.

We have seen that New Jersey is a state of many kinds of people from many other countries. They have learned to live together in spite of many differences and they have worked hard to make New Jersey a great state.

QUESTIONS

1. What are immigrants?
2. Why do people coming to the United States settle in New Jersey?
3. Before the War for Independence, from what three countries did people come to New Jersey?
4. Why did people leave Ireland to come to the United States?
5. Why did people from Italy, Poland, Hungary, Russia and Greece come to the United States?
6. What meaning and importance does the Statue of Liberty have to people coming to the United States to live?
7. Why was it often difficult for immigrants to find places to live and work?
8. What were three different types of jobs some of the immigrants did?
9. What made black immigrants different from other immigrants?
10. Why don't we have slavery in the United States today?

ACTIVITIES

1. Pretend you are an immigrant to New Jersey today. Describe how you would get food, a place to live and a job. You do *not* speak English but you may write your answer in English.

2. On a map of the United States, describe the route you might have taken if you were on the Underground Railroad.

ADVANCED RESEARCH

1. Investigate the customs of any two *ethnic* groups. Describe a few of their celebrations and what they are.
2. Investigate Harriet Tubman's life and experiences. Write a brief biography of a significant part of her life.

CHAPTER VII

Words you need to know

contribution	*cylinder*	*discouraged*
fame	*funnel*	*submerged*
idealist	*phonograph*	*periscope*
genius	*filament*	*orphanage*
stocks	*credit*	*eliminated*
practical	*generator*	
expensive	*dictate*	

INTERESTING PEOPLE IN NEW JERSEY'S HISTORY

New Jersey has been the home of many interesting and famous people. Some were born in the state and some came to it from other places. Many of these people made important *contributions* to the history of the state and the growth of the nation. We will look at the lives of a few of these people more carefully.

GROVER CLEVELAND

An American president was born in New Jersey. Grover Cleveland was born in Caldwell in 1837. The house in which he was born can still be seen in that town. While he was still a child his parents moved to New York. When he grew up he became a lawyer and was elected Governor of New York.

In 1884, Grover Cleveland was elected President of the United States. The President of the United States has a very difficult job, Grover Cleveland worked hard to do a good job as President. In 1892 he was elected President for a second time.

After finishing his second term as President, Grover Cleveland went back to New Jersey. He taught at Princeton University where he became friends with Woodrow Wilson who would later become a United States President. When Grover Cleveland died he was buried at Princeton in the state where he was born.

WOODROW WILSON

In 1875 a young man from Virginia began his studies at the College of New Jersey at Princeton. The college is today called Princeton University. The young man's name was Woodrow Wilson and he studied hard for four years. When he graduated from Princeton in 1879 he became a lawyer. After a few years he decided to become a teacher. He had been such a good student that he was asked to return to Princeton and to teach there. He taught history and law for several years and then he became President of the University.

As President of Princeton, Woodrow Wilson became well known for his honesty and his hard work. In 1910, the people of New Jersey elected him governor of the state. He became known as a person who made his own decisions. He would not allow others to tell him what to do if he thought they were wrong.

Woodrow Wilson's *fame* spread across the United States. In 1912 he was elected President of the United States. He became a very good President. For eight years he led the country through peace and war.

Woodrow Wilson is remembered as an *idealist*. An idealist is someone who believes that things can be made better. Woodrow Wilson worked hard to try to make changes in the way things were being done. He is still remembered for his honesty, his hard work, and his ideals.

THOMAS EDISON

Perhaps the most famous person ever to live in New Jersey was Thomas Alva Edison. Thomas Edison is sometimes called a *genius* because he invented so many things.

As a boy, Thomas Edison was always asking questions. In fact, he asked so many questions that his teachers thought he was trying to make trouble. His mother, who was a teacher herself, decided to teach him at home. Thomas never returned to school but he kept asking questions and learning. He set up his own workshop where he could experiment with the many ideas that came into his head. He used a type of discovery called trial and error. He would keep trying different ways of doing something until he found one that worked.

One of Thomas Edison's first inventions was a machine which told people the prices of *stocks* which were selling on the stock market. With the money he made from that invention he made a bigger workshop. He then found ways to make two other inventions better. He improved the typewriter and the telephone. He had decided that he would only work on things which were *practical*. Something is practical when it has a purpose and can be used to do something. Thomas Edison also wanted to be sure that the things he invented would not be too *expensive*. He wanted people to be able to afford to buy them.

In 1876, Thomas Edison set up a laboratory in Menlo Park, New Jersey. It was one of the first scientific research laboratories in the United States. Here he worked on his two most important inventions.

THE PHONOGRAPH

One day Edison handed a drawing of a machine to one of his helpers. With the drawing was a note which said, "make this." The helper obeyed and when he brought the finished machine to Thomas Edison he asked, "What will it do?" The inventor replied, "Oh, it is going to talk". The machine was nothing more than a *cylinder* with tinfoil wrapped around it. The cylinder looked like a tin can lying on its side. Attached to the cylinder was a *funnel* shaped mouthpiece. Into the mouthpiece Thomas Edison recited the poem, "Mary Had a Little Lamb". As he spoke, the cylinder on the machine was turned by a hand crank. When he had finished speaking he turned the cylinder back to its starting place. As he turned the crank again his voice could be heard saying, "Mary had a little lamb, its fleece was white as snow". The *phonograph* had been invented. Phonographs of today use records instead of cylinders. They are usually called record players or stereos and make a much clearer sound than did Thomas Edison's. But his was the first and the machines of today still use his basic idea.

THE ELECTRIC LIGHT

In 1879, Thomas Edison was working on another idea. He knew that an electric light which could burn for many hours would help people around the world to live and work very differently. The problem was to find the right kind of material from which to make a *filament*. The filament is the part of an electric light which glows when electricity is passed through it. Thomas Edison tried everything. He even tried the hair from a friend's beard. Everything he tried burned up too quickly. Finally, he took a piece of sewing thread and turned it into charcoal by burning it. Then he put it into a glass bulb in which there was no air. When the electricity was turned on the filament burned for nearly two days. Later the bulb was improved so that it would burn for several months. The electric light was now practical. Soon houses and buildings around the country were being lighted with electricity.

Thomas Edison later moved his laboratory to West Orange. There he worked for nearly fifty years. He has been given *credit* for inventing more than one thousand things during his life time. Most of his inventions were practical things which are still helping to make our lives easier and more enjoyable. These include improvements in the telephone, the electric *generator* and the electric storage battery. He also made the *dictating* machine and some of the first motion pictures. Our lives would be very different today without Thomas Edison's inventions.

JOHN HOLLAND

Have you ever been on board a submarine? At Hackensack you can visit a submarine from the days of World War II. It is a memorial to the men who have lost their lives in submarines. It can also be a reminder that a man from New Jersey was the inventor of the modern submarine.

John Holland was an immigrant from Ireland. In 1873 he came to live in Patterson, New Jersey. He had spent many years drawing plans for a boat which could sail under water. Most people thought John Holland was a little bit crazy. Submarines had been tried before but they had never really worked very well. John Holland refused to give up because he believed that the submarine would work and would be very important someday.

In 1878, John Holland built his first submarine and tried it on the Passaic River in Paterson. Unfortunately, it was too heavy. The first time it was put into the water it sank to the bottom and would not come to the surface. People said they knew it would not work but John Holland did not become *discouraged*.

Three years later John Holland had built a second submarine. It was thirty-one feet long and could carry three men. He called it the Fenian Ram. The Fenian Ram was tested in the waters of New York Harbor. It *submerged* one-hundred feet and stayed down for more than an hour before coming to the surface. John Holland had proved that the submarine could work. People still did not think the submarine had any value. Why would people want to sail around on the bottom of the ocean they asked. There was nothing to see there. Unfortunately, at that time they were right. From inside the Fenian Ram there was no way to see where you were going. This made the submarine very dangerous. One day it bumped into a ferry boat as it was coming to the surface and the submarine sank to the bottom. The men inside were rescued but the Fenian Ram was too badly damaged to be used again. Later, however, it was raised from the bottom. Today it can be seen in Westside Park in Paterson. It is a kind of memorial to John Holland.

Finally, another New Jersey inventor named Simon Lake invented the *periscope*. This allowed people inside the submarine to see above the water.

In 1898 John Holland built another submarine. Into it he put all of the improvements he had learned when making his earlier submarines. It also had a periscope. He called the submarine the Holland. The Holland worked so well that the United States Navy agreed to buy it. The Navy also asked John Holland to build some more submarines. He organized a company which is still building submarines for the Navy today.

John Holland had refused to become discouraged when people told him that his ideas would not work. He had continued to improve something that he knew would work. It had been difficult but he had succeeded. Today, thanks to John Holland, the submarine is one of the most important ships in the modern navy.

CLARA MAASS

Clara Maass was the oldest of eight children. Her father was a poor hat maker in East Orange. Clara was forced to work for food and a place to sleep by the time she was ten years old. At age fifteen Clara was working full time in a Newark *orphanage*. Most of her work was cleaning and washing but she enjoyed helping with the children when she got the chance. Then Clara learned that she could train to become a nurse at a Newark hospital. She worked hard and received her nurse's cap when she was eighteen.

As a nurse, Clara volunteered to serve with the army. In 1898 she worked in army camps in Cuba and later in the Philippine Islands. In these camps she treated many soldiers who were suffering from yellow fever. Yellow fever was a disease which killed thousands of people each year. It was most common in areas where the climate was moist and hot. Doctors thought that people got the disease after being bitten by mosquitoes but they were not sure. Experiments had to be done. People had to allow themselves to be bitten by mosquitoes which were known to have bitten other people with the disease.

Clara Maass wanted to help end the suffering which was caused by yellow fever. She volunteered to be one of the people bitten by the infected mosquitoes. A jar filled with mosquitoes was placed against her arm and they were allowed to bite her. Very soon afterward Clara had yellow fever. In August, 1901, Clara died from the disease. She had given her life but doctors now had the proof that they needed. A huge program to kill mosquitoes in Cuba and elsewhere was begun. As a result, few if any people get yellow fever anymore. The disease has been nearly *eliminated.* Clara Maass is remembered as a brave woman. She was willing to give her life so that the lives of many others could be saved.

OTHER FAMOUS NEW JERSEYIANS

New Jersey has so many people who have done things to make them famous it is hard to mention them all. We have already read about several inventors and scientists but New Jersey had many more. John Mason found a way to preserve food in a glass jar in order to keep it from spoiling. The jars which he used were called "Mason Jars". People still us them to preserve fruits and vegetables today.

Albert Einstein was probably one of the most intelligent men who ever lived. He discovered some very important things which helped scientists to answer questions about the beginning of our universe. Even though he did not like war it was his idea which led to the making of the first atomic bomb. Later he worked hard to see that his ideas would only be used for peaceful things. Albert Einstein came to this country from Germany. He spent his last years teaching and working at Princeton University.

New Jersey is a state with a long seacoast. Perhaps this is why some of the nation's best remembered naval heroes have come from the state.

Captain James Lawrence from Burlington was the commander of the warship Chesapeake during the War of 1812. In a bloody battle with a British ship off the coast of New England he was seriously wounded. Even though he was dying he was more concerned about winning the battle than saving his own life. As he was carried below decks he said to his crew, "Don't give up the ship". His words are still remembered as examples of loyalty and duty.

Captain Richard Somers of Somers Point won fame in another war. He volunteered to sail a small ship loaded with explosives into the harbor of a place called Tripoli. The Barbary Pirates of Tripoli had been attacking American ships and demanding money from them. Captain Somers was killed when the ship he was sailing exploded too soon. However, his brave deed helped to stop the pirates from bothering American ships.

Admiral William Halsey from Elizabeth was another naval hero. He was the commander of the American naval forces in the South Pacific Ocean during World War II. He was called the greatest fighting admiral of the war. His leadership helped the American navy to win some very important victories.

One New Jersey navy man is famous for his adventures in space rather than the ocean. He was one of America's first astronauts. Walter Schirra was born in Hackensack. His father was a pilot and he taught Wally to fly when he was a young boy. Wally became a pilot in the United States Navy after graduating from the United States Naval Academy. He flew airplanes and then volunteered to be one of the first astronauts. As an astronaut he piloted three different space crafts. He made a total of one-hundred and eighty-five trips around the earth. He was the first astronaut to link up with another craft in space. Walter Schirra's work helped to pave the way for the first landings on the Moon a few years later.

The list of famous and important people from New Jersey goes on and on. Peter McGuire, who lived in Camden, was the founder of Labor Day. Labor Day has become an important holiday which honors American workers. Thomas Nast, a famous cartoonist, lived in Morristown. It was Nast who first drew the donkey and the elephant which today stand for the Democratic and Republican Parties. James Marshall of Lambertville discovered a nugget of gold in a river in California in 1849. His discovery led to the famous California Gold Rush of that year. Clara Barton founded the American Red Cross. Dorothea Dix led a movement to improve the care for people who were mentally ill. Both of these women lived some of their lives in New Jersey. Willis Carrier made the first air conditioner. The company he founded still makes air conditioners in Newark.

Many important poets and authors have made New Jersey their home. They include, John O'Hara, Philip Roth, LeRoi Jones and William Carlos Williams.

Some of the nation's most popular entertainers have come from New Jersey. They include singer Frank Sinatra, comedian Jerry Lewis and actors Jack Nicholson and John Travolta.

Perhaps you know of other famous New Jerseyians. Maybe someday you or someone in your class will do something like one of these people we have been reading about. Then you will be among the many famous people who have called New Jersey home.

QUESTIONS

1. Which President of the United States was born in New Jersey?
2. Why did Woodrow Wilson come to New Jersey?
3. What three jobs did Woodrow Wilson have?
4. Why was Thomas Edison called a genius?
5. What does trial and error type of discovery mean?
6. Name three things Thomas Edison improved or invented.
7. Why would it have been easy for John Holland to be discouraged?
8. What was special about Clara Maass' contribution?
9. What may have helped New Jersey to have so many sea and navy heroes?
10. Who was Walter Schirra and what did he do?

ACTIVITIES

1. Draw a picture or make a collage which shows some of the inventions Thomas Edison made.
2. On a map of New Jersey, label the cities where the interesting people discussed in this chapter lived or worked.
3. Cut out and mount or draw the symbols of the Republican and Democratic Parties.

ADVANCED RESEARCH

1. Select one of the interesting people discussed in this chapter and find out more about that person. Write a report or give a talk to your class about the person you selected.
2. Thomas Edison was given credit for inventing more than one thousand things. How many can you list?
3. Research and report on how submarines submerge, float and move.

CHAPTER VIII

Words you need to know

fans	*capital*	*perils*
organized	*produce*	*audience*
goal	*studios*	*Premier*
defender	*scenery*	*requirements*
stadium		

HISTORY MAKING EVENTS IN NEW JERSEY

As we have seen, much history has been made in the State of New Jersey. In the years since the first settlers came to the state it has been the scene of many "firsts." Things which would later be done in many other places were done in New Jersey for the first time. Also, New Jersey's history is filled with many events and people who were important and interesting. Let us read about some of these things in greater detail.

HISTORIC SPORTING EVENTS

Do you like football and baseball? Today they are two of this country's most popular games. Millions of *"fans"* watch games played by professional and college teams across the United States. An important part of the history of both of these games begins in New Jersey. The first *organized* baseball game and the first college football game were both played in the state.

THE FIRST BASEBALL GAME

For most of our country's history baseball has been considered the nation's number one sport. The game from which baseball grew is believed to have first been played in England more than three-hundred years ago. The game was then called rounders. Rounders was a popular after-school game with children for many years. The players used a bat and a ball and they ran around bases just like in the game of baseball today. There were several ways to play the game but there was no written set of rules saying exactly how it should be played.

In the United States, clubs were formed for the purpose of playing rounders and interest in the sport grew. One such club was called the New York Knickerbockers. The members of the Knickerbocker club were well organized. They decided to write down the rules for the game and to play all of their games according to those rules.

Many of the rules which the Knickerbockers wrote down are still part of the game of baseball today. They include the shape of the field, the distance between the bases and the number of men on a team. They also decided that there would be three outs in each inning and that three strikes at the ball would be an out.

The Knickerbockers played their games at a place called the Elysian Fields in Hoboken, New Jersey. One day in 1846, another baseball club called the New York Baseball Club challenged the Knickerbockers to a game. The New York club was not as well organized as the Knickerbockers but they liked the rules by which the Knickerbockers played. One popular rule said that a batter could not be walked. He could let as many pitches as he wished go by until the pitchers threw him one that he liked. In other words, he could continue to bat until he hit the ball or struck out.

The game between the Knickerbockers and the New York Baseball Club was played in Hoboken on June 19, 1846. Many people came to the Elysian Fields to watch the game. They expected the better dressed and better organized Knickerbockers to win. But that was not the way it turned out.

The Knickerbockers had made the rules for the game but the New Yorkers had learned to play better. The final score was New York 23 and the Knickerbockers 1. Even though they lost the game the Knickerbocker's rules created a great interest in the game of baseball. Teams from all over the country asked for printed copies of their rules. They also copied the Knickerbocker's uniforms which looked something like the uniforms of baseball players today. The game of baseball became the most popular game in the country.

The next time you play or watch a game of baseball, remember that many of the rules which players must still follow were first used in that game played in Hoboken in 1846.

THE FIRST COLLEGE FOOTBALL GAME

The first football game between two colleges in the United States was played in New Brunswick, New Jersey in 1869. The teams were from the colleges of Princeton and Rutgers. If you had been there you might not have known what game they were playing. The field was very crowded.

There were twenty-five players on each side. Instead of the familiar football with points at both ends they used a round rubber ball something like the ball used in the game of soccer. The players scored points by kicking the ball across the other team's *goal* line. They could also hit the ball across with their fists. *Defenders* could try to stop the kicker by tackling him or knocking him to the ground. Each time the ball crossed the goal line it was worth one point.

The players did not wear helmets or other protective clothing. Sometimes players struggling for the ball formed huge piles of bodies with arms, legs and heads sticking out. It was a very rough game.

The game in New Brunswick was not played in a *stadium*. The people who came to watch had to stand along the sidelines or sit on a fence near the field. During one play a member of the Rutgers team crashed into the fence and the people came tumbling down.

The action on that long ago day was fast and furious. At one time in the game the score was tied with each school having four points. However, by the time the game ended Rutgers had scored two more times and won the game by a score of 6 to 4.

After the game both teams and their fans celebrated with a meal together. Like football fans today, most of their conversation was probably about the game.

Rutgers and Princeton continued to play football and other colleges also began to play games against each other. Today on Saturday afternoons in the fall, teams meet in games all over the nation. Football fans by the thousands jam into huge stadiums to watch the games. Afterwards, they too meet with friends to celebrate and talk about the game. Much has changed since that first game in New Jersey more than one hundred years ago, but much has stayed the same too.

MOTION PICTURES

Do you like to watch movies? Movies are made in many places today. One of the places many people think of when they think of making movies is Hollywood, California. Hollywood is still sometimes called, "the motion picture *capital* of the world." However, that was not always true. At one time, many years ago, the motion picture capital of the world was Fort Lee, New Jersey.

Many inventors are given credit for making motion pictures possible. Motion pictures are very complicated and the ideas of these inventors had to be combined and improved upon before pictures could be made to move and appear lifelike. We have already read about one of the people who played a part in the history of motion pictures. He was Thomas Edison. In his laboratory in West Orange he developed one of the first successful motion picture projectors. Before the projector was developed only one person at a time could watch a motion picture. The projector used light to shine or project moving pictures on a screen. This made it possible for many people to watch the movies at the same time.

Thomas Edison also started a company to *produce* motion pictures for sale. In 1903 this company made one of the first motion pictures that actually told a story. It was called The Great Train Robbery and it lasted only eleven minutes. The movie showed actors, dressed like cowboys, stopping a train and stealing money from the passengers. It also showed these "bad men" being chased and captured by the sheriff. The robbery was supposed to be taking place in the wild west but the action was really filmed along a railway in New Jersey.

Many of the actors who worked in the first motion pictures lived in New York City. Since Fort Lee, New Jersey was just across the Hudson River from New York City, many of the early movie makers decided that it would make a good place for their *studios*. For about ten years, Fort Lee was truly a movie capital. Many of the films were made inside large buildings called studios but some were made outdoors using New Jersey's *scenery*. One movie called, "The *Perils* of Pauline" was about a woman who was always getting rescued at the last minute from some frightening or dangerous situation. In one scene in the movie she was seen hanging from a branch over the huge cliffs called the Palisades on the New Jersey side of the Hudson River. Of course, as the *audience* cheered, she was rescued at the last minute so that she could be seen in another adventure movie.

Eventually, the movie makers moved their studios to California. They did this because the weather there was better for making movies outdoors all year around. People soon forgot that Fort Lee ever had anything to do with the movie business. However, New Jersey was really the first and Hollywood the second "movie capital of the world".

THE GLASSBORO SUMMIT

History sometimes happens in unlikely places. In 1967, the town of Glassboro, New Jersey received world wide attention for a few days. For three days Glassboro was the meeting place of the leaders of two of the most powerful nations in the world.

By 1967 the United States had grown to be very powerful since the days of the War for Independence. It had become a nation with interests in many other parts of the world. Another big nation which had interests around the world was the Soviet Union or as it is also called, Russia. The leaders of the United States and the Soviet Union often disagreed with one another. Neither country completely trusted the other and many people feared that this could lead to war between the two large nations.

In 1967 the leader of the Soviet Union, Alexei Kosygin, came to New York to make a speech at the United Nations headquarters there. The President of the United States,

Lyndon Johnson, wanted to talk to *Premier* Kosygin. He hoped that such a talk would help to work out some of the differences between the two nations. However, Mr. Kosygin was in New York and Mr. Johnson was in Washington, D. C. Neither leader wanted to travel all the way to meet the other. Their assistants looked at a map to try to find a place about half-way between New York and Washington where the two leaders could meet. The meeting place had to be quiet and safe. It had to have a place that was large enough for the two leaders and their assistants to stay. Glassboro was chosen because it met their *requirements.* On the campus of Glassboro State College there was a beautiful old house in which the meetings could take place.

Glassboro became a very busy place for the next few days. Thousands of workmen, newspeople and policemen arrived and worked all night to prepare for the meetings. Special telephone lines and equipment for television cameras had to be set up. When the leaders of two of the largest nations in the world meet, the rest of the world wants to watch.

For three days the two men met. Many of their meetings were private but every so often they would come to the door of the house and tell the rest of the world what they were talking about.

When the meetings finally ended the two leaders had not agreed on everything. However, they had shown the world that it was possible for their two nations to talk rather than fight. Later, other United States and Soviet leaders would meet for talks like these.

A few days later Glassboro was quiet once again. The people of Glassboro were proud that their town had been able to serve as the place for this peaceful meeting. It was another of the many events in history which have taken place in the State of New Jersey.

CONCLUSION

Historical events are not just things that happened a long time ago. Things that are happening now will be history someday. The Indians, colonists, soldiers and other people you have read about in this book probably did not think they would be in New Jersey history books. Several years from now, people may be reading about events you have seen or people you know. There is even the possibility that something you do will be written about in history books. History is real, it is living, and it is being made right now in your state of New Jersey.

QUESTIONS

1. What two organized sporting games were first played in New Jersey?
2. What did the New York Knickerbockers do for the game of baseball?
3. What two colleges played the first football game and where did they play?
4. What two differences are there between the way the first college football game was played and the way football is played now?
5. What was Fort Lee famous for?
6. What was Thomas Edison's part in motion pictures?
7. Why did Hollywood become the motion picture capital of the world?
8. Why was attention focused on Glassboro in 1967?
9. What was shown to the world at Glassboro?
10. When do historical events take place?

ACTIVITIES

1. Draw your own map of New Jersey. On your map locate and label your hometown, Glassboro, Princeton, New Brunswick, Hoboken and Fort Lee.
2. Make a collage that includes pictures of things, places, people or events which may be found in New Jersey.

ADVANCED RESEARCH

1. Many other interesting historical events have occurred in New Jersey. Select an event, research it and give or write a report on the event.

2. Through the use of newspapers, magazines or some other source of information, describe some recent event which might be found in a New Jersey history book fifty years from now. Write in your own words how the event may be described.